Warrior of the Silence

Tatterdemalion Blue

New Edition
Published by **Tatterdemalion** Blue in 2024

Words © John King 2024
Illustrations © John King 2024

A CIP catalogue record for this book is available from the British Library

Cover design and layout by **Tatterdemalion** Blue

ISBN 978-1-915123-08-4

Tatterdemalion Blue
71 Maxwell Place
Stirling
FK8 1JU

www.tatterdemalionblue**.com**

Warrior of the Silence

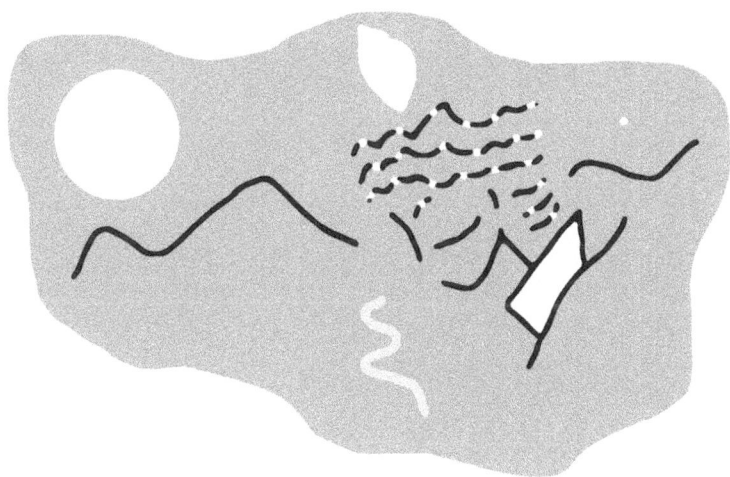

John King

This work is inspired by and dedicated to

* Shri Mataji Nirmala Devi *

~ *a journey to the beauty within* ~

For my sisters ...

Deanne ~ Katie ~ Helen

Contents

Imagine

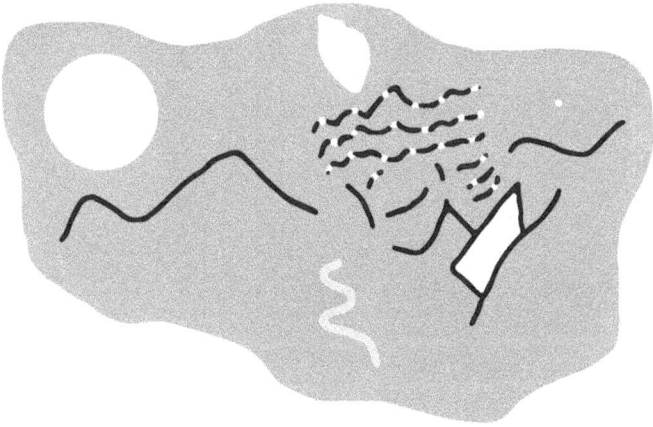

imagine if you will
a Gift

so precious - so real
it may enlighten the world

what if this Gift
is the treasure you seek?

what if it exists within
waiting to be awakened?

the warrior invites you
to share his journey

to share the realisation

of the beauty of the Gift
we have been given

The Light Within

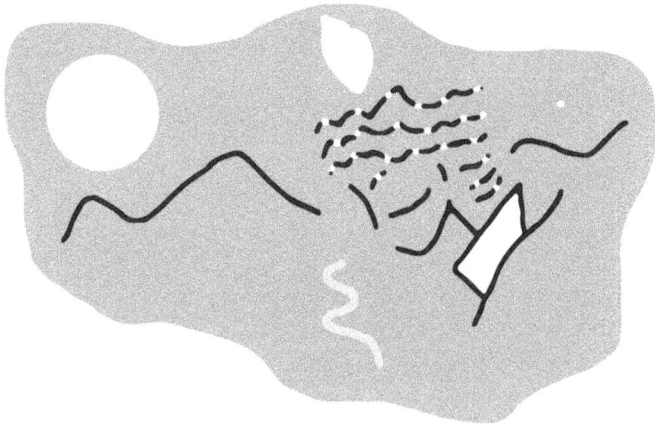

the sun is shining bright
but it is the light within that we must seek
to let shine

The Angel-Blessing

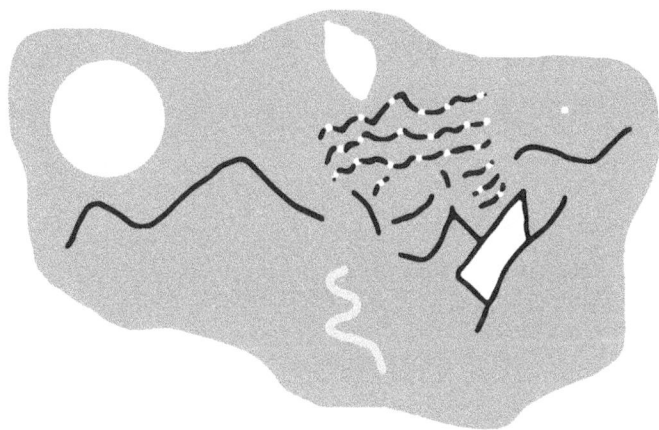

listen ...
will you listen to what I shall say to you?

from nowhere a voice
a calling?

I was alone upon the shore
I guess I was nowhere
but I was content with that
I was looking deep
deep into what lay beyond
deep into the heart of the mountains
the ocean and the skies

a gentle breeze was blowing
causing ripples of movement and sound
upon all that she touched

I was intent on listening
to what?

to everything
to nothing
to no-one
to my self

and I became less
as if all that was me
or I deemed to be me
ceased to exist

I was dissolving
fading until there was nothing
nothing at all
I was nowhere
nowhere to be found
and within that moment not a sound
all was silent
absolute Silence

the tiniest spark of a flame
arose
and I know not
if the spark was within me
or I was a witness
of the presence before me
for the deeper the Silence
the greater the flame

filling me beyond measure
with a light beyond words

for I was becoming the light

and the voice spoke so softly
such as beauty herself
so gently
I felt my being dissolve
dispersing this silent space

the less there was of me
the greater the calling

listen ...

She an Angel?

an Angel beyond words
for I was perceiving with senses
seeking perfection
and yet
how may I speak of my Angel?

She is realised
through the pure desire
to know the depths
of one's true being

the willingness
to be empty of all things
and be filled with the grace
of the Presence Divine

a blessing
illumined in the light
of the purest flame
breathing life
into all that She touches

awakening all
who will listen to Her voice
awakening all
who will listen to the calling

and if I may
I will share the words of my Angel ...

so long

I have been awaiting your return
for you have travelled so far from me

so near

did you see all that you desired to see?
did you hear all that you desired to hear?
did you feel all that you desired to feel?
did you come to know all that you desired to know?
did you travel the depths of your soul?

do you know me now?

for all that you desired to see
I have shown you

all that you desired to hear
I have spoken to you

all that you desired to feel
I have awakened within you

and all that you desired to know
I have revealed to you

upon your journey of the soul
I was your guide
I was your protection

do you see me now?

within your heart
do you hear me?

for your heart has been broken
and is being broken anew
that I may heal you

so you may feel me
and so you may know me

we are One

I exist as the pure desire of the heart
within
and without your being

I am the Angel-blessing
as you are a soul-saint

I am Love

will you not recognise me
when I call you?

how long must you stay away?

what was my reply I may not know

the words flowed from my heart
in silent longing

in silent communication

for there was no I
there was simply a light
that wished to burn so brightly
within the heart of another
and yet there was no other

the two were reflections
of the one light

I wondered of this
when
my communication ended

once more I was being filled
with a fear or sorrow

I was no longer filled with light
some of me had returned

the voice became fainter
and fainter

so far away
like a distant memory

listen ...

I lay down my head that I may sleep
praying I may dream of my Angel
that we may commune once more
and the light of the flame
may burn brightly in my heart

and while I slept She came to me

so silently She spoke my name
as from my dream I awoke
to find Her
in the Silence of my heart

listen ...

awakening
all was so clear

She was silence
and the source of the Silence

She was light
and the source of the Light

She was love
and the source that is Love

the flame illumined
within

and at one with my Angel
I walked from the shore
passing so many souls
and within the hearts of all
I perceived
the tiniest spark of a flame
burning so brightly
and the voice of their Angel
calling

and each shone such as my Angel
as if She were One
within every soul-saint

and yet
She shone in the aura of beauty
unique
to the presence of every soul
and I wished all to know
the beauty
of the Divine Light
that shone within them

that they may become the beauty
that they may become the light

that they may find their true self
within the depths
of the heart of the love of Love

She is so close

listen ...

will you listen to the calling?
will you listen
to what She shall say to you?

listen ...

Warrior of the Silence

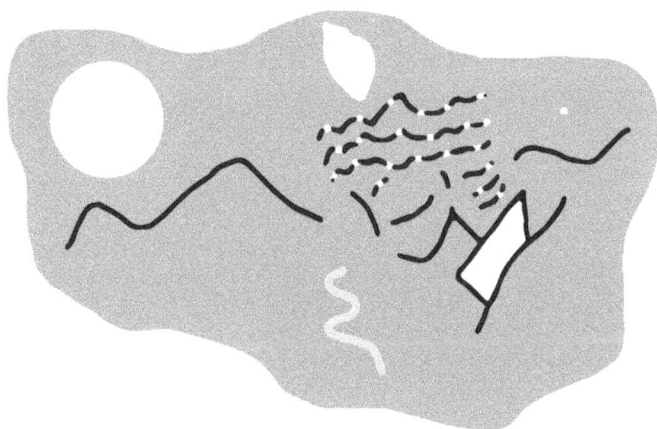

The Awakening

Awake

the sun shines bright this day
as a herald to the calling

the loving voice of the Mother
awakening Her children
to the inner grace of the Presence Divine

Her voice is like a silent rainfall
showering Her children
with manifold blessings
as they ascend their journey's resolve
for cleansed
in Her tender grace-showers
they too may shine bright like the sun
lighting the way as angels
saints and seekers

Her voice pervades all
a whisper on the breath of the breeze

all is light
all is life
all is love

Her voice is so clear

Awake

The Songbird Sings

the songbird
sings her sweet song
in the morning-glow
of moon-sun-light
the melody
beckoning the warriors

seek me in the Silence

a silent rainfall falls
filling the hearts
of the children
of the Mother of Creation

they are One

an emanation of the flame
lit as a beacon
on every horizon

the melody is for all

the songbird
sings her sweet song
in the morning-glow
of a new day
dawning

He Is This

the essence
of this life
is his light
the beauty
of this world
is his dreaming
the wisdom
of this moment
is his waking self
the mystery of love
is his imagination
the way before him
is his ascending
the journey
is his soul seeking
the sun's radiance
is his guide
the moon illumined
is his reflection

the warrior
is communing
in eternity

in every way

he is this

Light-Dancing

morning rays
touch the ripples of the river-flow
light-dancing
transient like his life
memories appear and fade
in his surrender
to the whim of the wave
guiding his soul-vessel
on his journey to the ocean
She is before him
She is so close
and he must let go of all the things
that have bound him
that in his freedom he may fly
fleeting like the light
the sacred waters cleanse
and nurture his being
as the Gift of the ocean draws near
there are no thoughts
there are no wishes
only the pure desire of his self
to enter Her silent depths
he closes his eyes
as a witness of the beauty within
for soon with his eyes open
he will enter the ocean
light-dancing

The Ocean

Grace

grace falls as sacred showers
upon a silent
shimmering ocean
radiating rainbow hues
for the lost children
of the Most Holy Spirit
She
the Mother
showering Her blessings
upon all those seeking their home
within the heart of the source
of all creation

the waters fall
saturating the senses
in light cascading
filling the cups of all
who will empty themselves
of their illusory worlds
and be imbued with the grace
of a world hailing infinity
which has no beginning nor end
but exists simply because it is
a kingdom of heavenly bliss

the Divine Presence
of the eternal present

The Silent Wave

there is a flow
such as a silent wave
a ripple
on the still blue ocean
dispelling all doubts and all fears
cleansing all souls of the illusion
descending the depths
that the heights may be attained
by all those who
guided by the Silence may gaze
upon the distant shore
of the great ocean
for all may journey the waters
through the grace of the silent wave
whose sojourn is of the soul
whose desires dissolve
within the all pervading power
of the eternal flow of love

the wave is the guide of the way

it is light
it is truth

it is the essence of creation
borne of the flow
of the sacred waters of life

The Dust-Red Road

alone
upon the dust-red road
of the seeker
he dreams
as he dives the depths
of the silent ocean

and he arises
dust-red
in the veil of innocence
as he yields
to the unfolding petals
of the sacred flower
revealing
the light of the flame
in his heart

he is One
with the Silence

the ineffable resounding
his soul sojourn

the dust-red road
is his home
on his journey of the depths
of the silent ocean

Silent Like The Ocean

he is still

silent like the ocean

grace
like a melody flows
as a composition
of the petals
of the sacred flower
unfolding

awakening in him
the beauty
of the Presence Divine

a song so silent

so sublime
his eyes fill
with tears of joy
luminous in the light
of the brilliant flame
of his becoming

and he is still

silent like the ocean

The Breath of the Breeze

A Voice Like A Silent Whisper

the waters of the eternal stream
flow like a melody

and he listens to the beauty
of the Silence within

the ineffable

borne
of the breath of the breeze

and his heart his guide
he enters
the flowing waters
diving
the mystery depths
to arise
and witness
the bright white sands
of his becoming

and he listens

to a voice
like a silent whisper

we are One

Butterfly Wings

a gentle breeze blows
fluttering leaves
and floating petals

light like
butterfly wings
golden
against the sunrise

the breath of the breeze
calling
for the warriors
to awaken
and with their hearts
sing silent
in their wishes

for their wishes
are a cascade of joy
showering the world
with fluttering leaves
and floating petals

light like
butterfly wings
golden
against the sunrise

In Awe Of The Calling

the breath of the breeze
breathes silently
through
the sacred flute

and he is composed
of the melody

of every nuance
singing
of this
his soul sojourn

his being rejoices

light-dancing
the ripples
of the silent wave
guiding
his awakening

and he shines
bright
like the sunrise

eyes shimmering
in awe of the calling

A Perfect Sunrise

he stands resplendent
in the glory
of the rays
of the sun and moon
the light cascading
robe-golden raiment
revealing the depths
of his soul desire
aflame
like a perfect sunrise

the breath of the breeze
is calling

and he glides lightly
the wave of the ocean
to commune
with the angels
saints and seekers
gathered upon the shore

it is ours to know

it is our time to grow
within
the all pervading
beauty of love

The Journey

The Power Of The River-Flow

the power of the river-flow
is unstoppable

the pure desire to know
cascades
like a waterfall
seeking its source

the warrior yields
to the whim
of the wave
flowing
on the river
to the ocean
where
he will commune
as a child of the light

his gaze follows the flow

the essence of love
now a torrent of grace
for the seeker

his journey is home
upon
the power of the river-flow

A Soul-Saint Of Reality

he dances the dance of angels
light like the morning sunrise
borne
upon wisp clouds and silent rains

his illumined heart his guide
he steps from the dance
to walk sandy shores
and glittering oceans
light-rays falling
to touch him where he steps

loosing his clothing
he dives into the oncoming waves
splashing all around him
and swims deep within
seeking naught
but the Silence of his wishes

he rises from the waters
cleansed of the illusion
sprinkled light-fall gracing his gaze

he dances the dance of angels
light like the morning sunrise

a soul-saint of reality

The Child In His Mother's Eyes

the dust-red road is his home
his life embracing
protecting
and guiding
like a Mother to a child

every moment of every day
is scattered on the wind

and the transience
of each passing moment
is captured
in every particle
of red dust
rising
to reveal
the beauty within

he is One with his self
with the infinity he sees
sketched
upon every moment

the dust-red road is his home
clothing him in innocence
as a child
in his Mother's Eyes

A Spiralling Soul Ascent

cloud-shoes
journey
cloud-skies

sun-illumined wisps
light the way
of he
a soul-journeyman
a seeker of the Silence

cloud-shoes swirl
in a spiralling
soul ascent
and his flight
is light in life

a leaf of the tree
seeking its roots

he surrenders
it is all he can do
smiling inside
light-dancing

cloud-shoes
gracing
cloud-skies

The Tree of Life

The Garden Of Eden

may we recall the silent garden
the abode of the Tree of Life
swathed
in the celestial rays
of the sun and moon
arising
within and without
this heavenly realm
where no shadow of darkness
exists

may we recall being gathered
from the garden
to transpire
as fragrant flowers
each as beautiful as the next
for all must transpire
within the nature
of their unique beauty
and in that moment
may we seek to know
of the love of the life
we have been given
that the blossoming petals
of the flower of perfection
may simply be a reflection
of the Garden of Eden

That That He Sought

the Tree of Life
is evolving
the warrior
to be
all
that he must be

to speak
and to see

to listen
to the breath of the breeze

to become One

an emanation
of grace
dissolving
within
the light
of the flame
until

he becomes
naught
but that
that he sought

Wind-Walking The Tree Of Life

beneath the great bough
of the mighty tree
he dreams
a walker of the wind
breezing reality
and he gazes
from his waking self
musing the silent path

the dust-red road of the seeker

leaves fall in golden showers
like a blessed rainfall
and all is silent save the breeze

he listens

a silent whisper is calling
to all that he seeks to be

it was not so long ago
it was not so far away

the eternal stirs within
and he answers
the calling
wind-walking the Tree of Life

The Fruit Of The Tree

the Tree of Life
stands
gracious
and all-powerful

the roots flow ever deeper
and deeper
as leaves fall
where
the warriors gather
to commune the wisdom
of their calling

the tree feeds their hunger
and quenches their thirst
and they stand
strong
like the towering limbs
and flowing branches
heralding
a new day dawning

the tree rains grace-showers
and the warriors
resplendent
in the aura of the flame
bear fruit

The Warrior

Soul-Lights Of The Eternal Flame

a solitary flame
emblazoned on the horizon

a gathering

a communion of souls
whose individual flame
burns
like a candle in the night
yet as One
pales the sun and moon
to mere shadows

the presence eternal
is awakened within all
and they stand
bold
like the mountain majesty
which no force
may rend asunder

for theirs is the promise
of the glory of love
that will fill this world
with an illumined dawn

soul-lights of the eternal flame

A Seeker Of The Silence

he is a seeker of the Silence
a warrior of the red dust
rising
in memory of his passing
gazing on white clouds
gliding blue skies
like he a soul-journeyman
gliding the way
he is communing
with all around him
he is growing
living and dying
to be reborn as a reflection
of the new day dawning

he is the light of the sunrise
the depth of the ocean
the stillness of blue skies
the journey of white clouds
borne on a hidden breeze
he is the yielding
of the grasses and wild
the unique beauty
of the flower in the field
he is all of these and more
he is growing
he is growing

The Mystery Unfolding

the mystery is unfolding

the blossoming petals
of the sacred flower
bloom

and he appears fragile
beaten
by the torrent of the storm
that awoke him
from his dreaming self

a silent rainfall
falls
cleansing
healing
illumining his senses
that he may know
that he may grow
powerful
within the numinous
depths of his being

he is a warrior

an emanation of the grace
of the mystery unfolding

Rays Of The Morning Sunrise

the skies rain light-showers
dissolving the illusion

soon reality will shine
like a beacon on every horizon

the warriors are gathering
silent footsteps on the shore
souls in wonder
honing their weapon of love
for all who may witness
the glory innate
within their seeking self

for they will commune
in a voice so silent
all hearts will sing
and the music will hail infinity

the sacred waters are flowing
guiding every soul
to the ocean
to enter Her healing depths
for it is the moment
to shed the raiment of ignorance
and be dressed anew
in the rays of the morning sunrise

The Silence

The Petals Unfold

the petals unfold
in the beauty of creation
revealing for all
the flower of perfection

the Gift to life

a silent melody
awakening all
to the divinity within
where they may shine
in the light
of the eternal flame

each a soul-saint
each
an emanation of grace
here
and now

the petals unfold
in the beauty of creation

a composition
of a new song of songs
resounding the depths
of the Silence

Sacred Flower

petals of the sacred flower
adorn the earth
borne
of the grace of angels
guiding the seekers' ascent
for each
will be composed
of rainbow hues
and pure fragrant blessings
raising all
to a unique kingdom
beyond this
their soul sojourn

and with each breath
of the breeze
another petal will unfold
revealing the depths
of the beauty within
as grace-showers
like a silent rainfall
fall
calling from within
the Silence
to rise as One

as petals of the sacred flower

Silence Breaks Upon The Shore

Silence breaks upon the shore
of every soul seeking
the glory of their perfection
the ebb and flow a reminder
of the presence here before us
for all may enter the ocean
in a unique discovery
of the silent depths within
and arise alive
to this most special time

the silent waters
will cleanse and nourish
revealing our true being
and through the grace
of the flame
will awaken the world
to the beauty
of the Gift She has given

warriors of the Silence

the fruition
of the sacred Tree of Life

Silence breaks upon the shore
of every soul seeking

A Soul-Vessel Entering Eternity

his soul-vessel glides silent waters
of reflection
the sun and moon as guides

ripples skim the surface to splash
the bright white sands of distant shores

memories of fleeting footsteps
returning to the ocean

the mirrored tree
scattered in his passing is born anew
as a soul-white dove graces his gaze
beckoning his freedom flight

a silent rainfall falls
adorning the world before him

he is all of these
destiny portrayed within his silent depths
and he shines as light inside
the emblazoned flame of his soul desire

all is as it is
as it will be

a soul-vessel entering eternity

Beauty

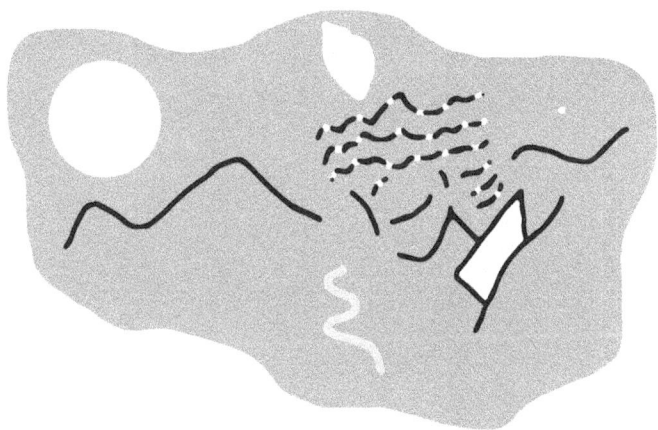

from the Silence of my heart
the depths of the silent ocean
a voice spoke

my son
in the Silence what may you see?

I perceived a tiny flame
burning so brightly
within the heart of hearts
a vision
such as the birth of the light of love
that shone in the aura of reflection
of the Divine Mother alone
eternal
eternally known
the essence of the flame
and the source of which exists
within the heart of every being
that they too may shine in the light
of the eternal presence within
all suns and moons and planets
all galaxies and universes
spiralling the light that exists
simply because it is
and to the question I answered

Beauty

from the Silence of my heart
the depths of the silent ocean
the voice spoke

my son
in the Silence what may you hear?

I listened in innocence
and through the wisdom discerned
a fountain of light
whose inner majesty pervaded creation
with a sound such as silent rainfall
and every drop of rain was a voice
the voice of an angel
saint or seeker
together
singing in the Silence
for every soul upon hearing this sound
found life
and their hearts so full of love
in joy resounded creation
with a new song of songs
now
but one voice
singing so silently in Silence
and to the question I answered

Beauty

from the Silence of my heart
the depths of the silent ocean
the voice spoke

my son
in the Silence what may you feel?

aware of no feeling I was nowhere
nowhere to be found
for only
in the nothingness of my being
could I be filled
and within that moment
the flowing waters of the sacred ocean
showered upon me
drenching my senses in rose-petal rain
cleansing and healing my being
swathed
in the light of the flame
that shone within my heart
filling the illimitable
until most surely my being dissolved
the senses as One
absorbed within the depths
of the Silence
and to the question I answered

Beauty

from the Silence of my heart
the depths of the silent ocean
the voice spoke

my son
in the Silence what may you know?

within the Silence
was a child in innocence
and the child was I as I was the child
innocence
the secret of the sacred path
that leads to Her door
for She is waiting
guiding Her children home
that She may raise them
to their illumined heights
that they may know of the source
of the flame
burning so brightly within their hearts
and through the vision perceived
they may witness their life
as a child in innocence
innocence
the wisdom of the Silence
and to the question I answered

Beauty

from the Silence of my heart
the depths of the silent ocean
the voice spoke

my son
and in the Silence what is beauty?

through the Gift
of the eternal presence
borne
of the light of the flame
the beauty shone
within my heart

in Her Silence
and in Her Sound

of the form
and of the formless

and through the grace
of She
the Most Holy Mother
my being at One
with the source of the Silence
to the question answered

Love

The Flower of Perfection

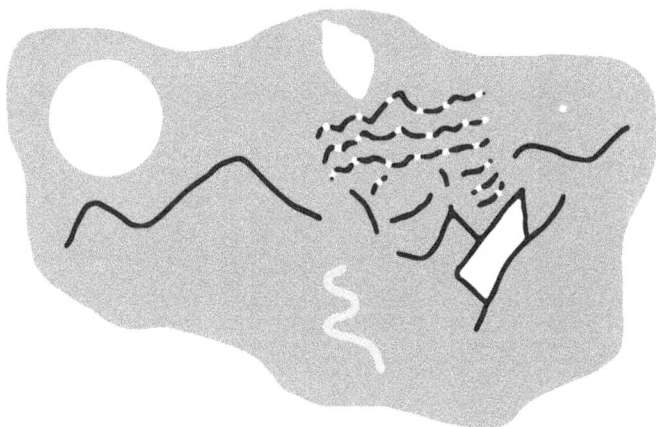

I was alone upon a crossroads
four directions - one decision to make
I perused the distance before me
but in whichever way I chose to look
the sun and the moon shone above me
on either side of the horizon

had I journeyed one of these roads?
if so
I no longer knew which one

seeking my repose
I sat down on the place where all roads met
and closing my eyes to gaze inside
I drifted awhile in contemplation

upon opening my eyes there appeared before me
a bright shining soul smiling in light
I rubbed my eyes feeling that I was dreaming
but when I opened them still he shone before me
and if I looked closely he looked a little like me

words of light appeared to emanate his heart

She awaits you ...

his Silence spoke

She?

what do you seek?

what do I seek?

for so long I had been searching

through all my lives' journeys
and in all my silent dreaming
so many times I failed to heed the signs
which had left me a little broken
a little lost
yet the first time I saw Her I knew
my heart rejoiced and my soul desire
was to dive the depths of Her Silent Ocean

my wish was granted
the drop became the ocean
grace like a fountain showered upon me
filling me completely
with a love that knew no bounds
cleansing
healing
nurturing my being until
She the Mother and I the child became One
all seemed so clear and I wished for all
to share the Gift of Her Love

I thought I had discovered the key to my soul
yet here I stood upon a crossroads

there exists a fountain of light
whose shimmering majesty
radiates the most holy colours
of the sacred rainbow
magnificent
in Her most perfect reflection
of the divinity within
and this fountain may shower light
upon all who seek Her
upon all who seek the glorious font
of all knowledge
flowing from the eternal
for once this fountain is known
all may bathe amidst
the cascading showers
of brilliant light
cleansing
nurturing
raising each soul to their own throne
as a witness of the source
of the roots of all creation
for the Tree of Life
may bloom within all
perceived as simply
the most perfect reflection
of the divine shimmering majesty
of the fountain of light

the words seemed to sound in my heart
like a silent heartbeat

what do you seek?

his Silence touched me deeply
what do I seek?

She awaits you ...
do you recall the tree?

the tree?

he took from his pocket a seed
a golden seed so bright
the sun and the moon appeared to fade

and he threw the golden seed
high into the air
where she shone
sprinkling dust-light all around
like a fountain of light
which upon touching the earth
arose as a mighty tree
from the place where all roads met

in awe of this vision
I lay down upon her roots
to rest awhile in her calm embrace

my shining soul sat down beside me
and from my heart's longing I asked
please tell me of the tree

he smiled
and the Silence of his heart
spoke to me these words ...

far away in a wondrous land
a land we have almost forgotten
there flowers a tree

the Tree of Life

for of the tree all things were born
and to the tree
all things must return
for the tree has stood forever
and will stand forever
beyond the limits of time itself

you see for her there is no time

before ever we were
or ever we will be she blooms

and if for a moment you close your eyes
you may catch a glimpse of her
swathed in eternal bloom

imagine if you will
a magical forest
filled with all the beauty
of the imagination

picture if you will
a circular clearing
a sunlit meadow-glade
graced in shape and hue
with the most fragrant of flowers
which
with every breath of the breeze
sends ripples
of colour and sound
on waves of fragrance
to reach us
wherever we may be

a sound
like a silent whisper
calling for us
to return
to this wondrous place

for once the many peoples
encircled the tree
living together in harmony

at one with creation

in the centre of the meadow-glade
stands a hill
upon which blossoms
the Tree of Life
so wide that it may take days
or weeks or years
to complete the circle
so high that the flowers and fruits
appear to be the stars themselves
adorning the heavens

on one side is the sun
on the other side the moon

while the moon rests
so the sun illumines the day
bringing light
and life to the earth

while the sun is witness
so the moon illumines the night
bringing rest
and sleep and dreams

the light emanates the tree
and through the sun and the moon
pervades creation

the tree is light

if you look closely
you may see white clouds
offering their wishes
in showers of rain
or snowflakes dancing
on the branches and leaves
and the fruits
of the tree

the time is eternal
the tree's branches are awash
with russet-red
auburn-orange
emerald-green leaves
and the many colours
of the ripened fruit

some seem ready to fall
and if they do it appears
that some distant constellation
has ceased to exist
descending the heavens
to the earth
to nourish
and be nourished by the tree

to be reborn of the seed

the tree is life

if you listen carefully
you may hear
the sacred waters flowing

the sound of the rivers
and streams
on their journeys
to the sea
and to the ocean

listen

the sound seems
to emanate the tree

the waters appear to flow
through the branches and leaves
while the ripened fruit
fills the heavens
with suns and moons
and stars and planets

all is clear

and if you look closely
you may see
the shimmering colours
of the sacred rainbow
sent to adorn creation

look carefully
someone sits before the tree

for if on your journey
you approach
from any side at any time
look closely
and you will see Her
sitting so peacefully still

for to see Her
is to wish to be before Her
on lush grass and springy moss
knowing you are home

for it is said
She has existed forever
just like the tree

it is said
She existed before the tree
and there will come a time
when all will be absorbed
within Her Silent Depths

some say She is the tree
through which Her Love manifests

the tree is love

some call Her
the Mother of Creation

the Divine Mother
who awaits the return
of all Her children
from their many wanderings
for Her Love is illimitable
and flows
through the branches
and leaves
and the ripened fruit
through which all
may know life

Her poise is peace
Her smile
illumines the heavens
with a light emanating love

for although She moves not
through the tree She oversees all
from the deepest depths
to the highest heights
no thing is overlooked
but simply shines
as Her most perfect reflection

She awaits Her children

once all Her children sat
where now the flowers grow
each one a reflection
of the child who departed

for long ago
as Her children
sat before Her
the breath of the breeze
sent ripples
through the branches
and the leaves of the tree

the voice of the Mother
communing
with each child
the wisdom of their calling

they listened as one
and at peace with all things
they returned to their homes
within the forest
until
one day
as they bathed in the light
of the tree
She raised Her hand
and seven ways appeared
to lead them through the forest

from that moment
they no longer perceived the tree
but wandered a little lost
and a little confused
until each chose their path to follow

they followed the ways
that led them through the forest
to bright sandy shores
and brilliant blue oceans
upon which great ships
with white sunlit sails
awaited
to carry them to distant lands

each taking their place
on the roots of the tree

seven wonders were born
around which arose
seven supreme realms
for the memory of the tree
was still very much alive
in their lives

the mighty roots
flowing through the earth
to nurture
guide and protect

for the memory of the tree
remained

in the light in the eyes
in the flight of the bird
in the petals and leaves
of the flowers and trees
in the hills and valleys
mountains and seas
in moon-sun-light
and candle light
for those who may wish to see

in the songs and stories
in the breeze that blows
in evensong and birdsong
in the sound of rain and snow
in the waters of waterfalls
streams and oceans
in the storms and silence
for those who may wish to hear

in the heat of the sun
in the cool of the moon
in the snow and the rain
in the wind and the still
in the breath of the breeze
in all of these
for those who may wish to feel

*in the stars and planets
and the constellations
in symbols and signs
and dreams and awakenings
in joy and laughter
and the grace of nature
for those who may wish to know
of the Presence Divine*

*for in the beginning
the knowledge of the tree
was known and passed on to all
and all revelled in listening
to the wisdom of the wise
and when it was time
aware of the way
each soul returned to the tree*

this was a golden time

*but as the ages passed
the knowledge of the tree
became less and less
for though
the wisdom shone
in the hearts of the wise
many departed the seven realms*

only a few returned

the knowledge of the tree dispersed
becoming but a distant memory
in the hearts and minds
of the people

disharmony arose
the people began to mistrust
the words of the wise
and they began to separate
becoming fearful of nature
of the myriad creatures
of one another
and of themselves

realms and kingdoms rose and fell
and almost all remnants of the tree
became lost in the dust and rubble
of ancient ruins

the wise came less and less
for if they spoke of the tree
they were shunned
and forced to leave the lands
to seek the solace
of the mountains and forests

some people began to misuse
the knowledge of the tree
to seek power over others

creating replica trees
to deceive those
who sought the truth
into following falsehoods
and to lead the seekers
farther and farther
from their true path

and yet
while there was much confusion
still
the memory prevailed
for in the midst of uncertainty
would appear

a flower
a ripened fruit
a falling leaf
a thunder-burst and lightning
a white cloud
a drop of rain
a snowflake dancing
a bird on the breeze
it may be the taste of spring
a winding road
a friend's return
a light in the eyes of the wise
a Mother's love
a smile in the eyes of a child

still the wise came
to awaken the calling
they were still and fleeting
but their message was eternal
for if in the Silence
you were still
you could enter eternity
and perceive the way before you

and now once more
the way before us is clear
that all who so desire may find Her

his words sang in my heart
like a memory
a melody of song sung so long ago
calling to me
from the depths of ages

She awaits you ...

my eyes were open
before me my bright soul shone
the tree was no more
but if I closed my eyes
I perceived her within me

her roots seeking
the hidden depths of my being

from within his heart
my shining soul revealed a flower
of ethereal splendour
and I was in awe of her beauty

he raised the flower
to the heavens
sprinkling dust-light
all around
and in a moment of grace
he bowed low
and laid her gently
at the centre of the crossroads
where illumined in bloom
she arose

a great ocean appeared
so silent
so still
reflecting her perfection
and the four roads became
but four streams of light
flowing
on their journeys of eternity

do you recall the flower?

I felt I did as from within my heart
his Silence spoke as mine

once upon the journey
of the sacred path
I gazed upon
a wondrous sight

a silent garden
illumined in the light
of grace-showers
falling all around
and from within
I espied
the most beautiful flower
shining
in the splendour and glory
of the light of perfection

and in this moment
as I witnessed this vision
I was absorbed
within Her silent depths
where She spoke to me
these words

my son
why must you still wander so?

rest awhile
within the unfolding petals
of love's fragrant embrace

for upon your journey
you have been
like the flower
who when the sun shone
sought the shade
who in the moonlight
wept
crying silently alone

who when it rained
sought shelter
lest in your eyes
your pain be known
and who when it snowed
so afraid of being stained
by life
hid your soul's
golden raiment

but most of all who
when the breath of the breeze
blew
breathing your name
covered your ears
lest you may hear the calling

my son
know the flower exists
within you

know that you may shine
bright
like the sun
and may reflect upon
your journey as the moon

know that your tears
may fall
as grace-showers
all around you
and know
that when it rains
you will be eased of all pain

know that the snowflakes
may dance with you
carpeting the way
of your footsteps
and when
the breath of the breeze blows
dispelling all doubts
and all fears
listen within the Silence
and you may enter the garden
to be awakened in eternity
in silent soul reflection

for I have always been with you
as the flower of your perfection

I opened my eyes
to perceive the flower
radiant
as the flame in my heart

and I realised
that on all of my journeys
in all of my searching
I had been seeking

the Flower of Perfection

for it was not until
I had ceased
from my wandering
and stood still
within
the Silence
that She could be found

Her reflected light
shining
within and without
my being

She in whose eyes
I may see
the silent beauty
of my soul

She lights my days
She illumines my nights
for the flower
of this love for Her
in me
bears the fruit
of the seed of eternity

and She blooms
enfolding Her fragrance
within
the uniquely sculpted
petals of creation
sown within
the hidden depths
of my being

and as I gaze
on the light of Love
blossoming
the flowering petals
of my heart
I see Her in me
and in me I see Her
as the most beautiful flower
in eternal bloom

Her fragrant petals
unfolding

his Silence spoke once more

there are so many souls awakening
in the bloom of the garden
each a unique petal of the sacred flower
blossoming in eternity

he plucked from the ocean the flower
and cradling her gently within his hands
he raised her to the heavens
as if offering the Gift to the world

he smiled and touched her to my heart
and my heart was filled with joy
for she shone
as the flower of the flame
within me

he raised her once more to the heavens

fragrant petals
on the wings of Silence flew
and I was a witness of eternity
as from beyond the firmament
petals fell like starlight
upon the ocean
and I entered Her Silent Depths

in finding Her I had found my Self

The Mother

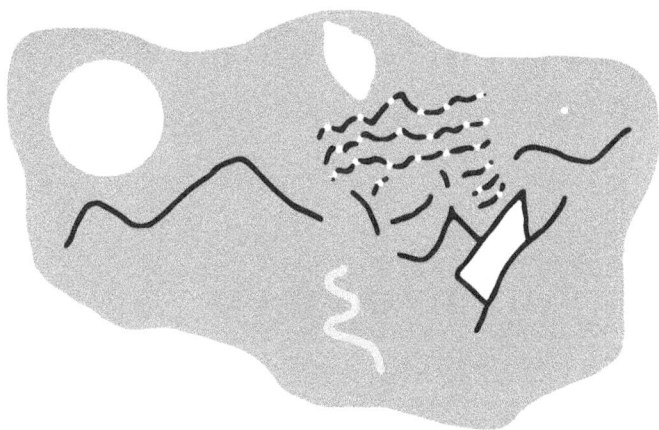

the Silence
ineffable

a silent whisper

I am here

and all of nature resounds
in answer to the calling
the breath of the breeze rustles
the branches and leaves
of the Tree of Life
in recognition of the Presence Divine
and every creature arises
alive to this most special time

it is the moment to be blessed
tender grace-showers
falling so silently
filling the cups of the angels
saints and seekers
for Her voice as truth speaks

of light
of life
of love

within the Silence
ineffable